MOMENTS OF
REVOLUTION

MOMENTS OF
REVOLUTION
EASTERN EUROPE

PHOTOGRAPHS BY
DAVID AND PETER TURNLEY
TEXT BY MORT ROSENBLUM

STEWART, TABORI & CHANG

NEW YORK

Text copyright © 1990 Mort Rosenblum

Photographs copyright © 1990 David C. Turnley, Peter Turnley, and the National Geographic Society, as noted specifically on pages 182 and 183, which constitute an extension of this page.

Published in 1990 by
Stewart, Tabori & Chang, Inc.
575 Broadway, New York, New York 10012

Library of Congress Cataloguing-in-Publication data
Turnley, David C.
  Moments of revolution : photographs of
  eastern Europe / by David and Peter Turnley ;
  text by Mort Rosenblum.
  184 pp.
    ISBN 1-55670-167-5
    ISBN 1-55670-168-3 (pbk.)
    1. Europe, Eastern—History—1945-
  1989—Pictorial works.
  I. Turnley, Peter. II. Rosenblum, Mort.
  III. Title.
  DJK50.T87 1990
  947.085—dc20   90-34861
                      CIP

Distributed in the U.S. by Workman Publishing, 708 Broadway, New York, New York 10003

Distributed in Canada by Canadian Manda Group, P.O. Box 920 Station U, Toronto, Ontario M8Z 5P9

Distributed in all other territories by Little, Brown and Company, International Division, 34 Beacon Street, Boston, Massachusetts 02108

Design by Diana M. Jones
Printed in Japan
10 9 8 7 6 5 4 3 2 1

PAGES 2 AND 3:
PRAGUE—*In an opening wave of their November revolution, a sea of Czechoslovaks floods the streets, under proud colors.* (DT)

PAGES 4 AND 5:
BUDAPEST—*Music erupts into politics at a Hungarian rock concert.* (DT)

PAGES 6 AND 7:
EAST BERLIN—*If the Eastern European revolution was sparked by workers, it was brought to the streets by students and young professionals. At Berlin's Gethsemane Church, candles light the first steps toward popular uprising.* (DT)

PAGES 8 AND 9:
BUCHAREST—*A Romanian insurgent shows the flag, Communist emblem ripped from the center, from the balcony where Nicolae Ceausescu fled two days before.* (DT)

PAGES 10 AND 11:
BERLIN—*A jubilant East German rides the wall near Potsdamer Platz.* (PT)

FRONTISPIECE:
BUCHAREST—*At Palace Square, young soldiers rally to a new banner, a Romanian flag with the hated Communist symbol torn out. Their defection signaled triumph for the revolution.* (PT)

PAGES 16 AND 17:
PRAGUE—*The spirit of Czechoslovak youth proved buoyant beyond expectation in the fall of 1989.* (PT)

CONTENTS

MOMENTS OF
REVOLUTION
Mort Rosenblum

Czechoslovaks jingled their keys in the air, and forty-one years of Communist Party totalitarianism fell away before their eyes. East Germans awoke one morning to find their hated wall had crumbled beneath its own weight. Romanians fought a bitter war against terror in their streets, but it was over in a week. From the Baltic to the Balkans, in a matter of months, the earth shifted. The words *freedom* and *democracy* were repeated again and again. But this was not about words.

Zdenek Machon was among a quarter-million Czechoslovaks who, on a December Sunday too cold for standing still, came back one more time to Wenceslas Square. He stood in a vast sea of arms outstretched in victory. Like the others, he made a triumphant V with his fingers. But he could not quite manage the national anthem. His voice cracked and boiled over from the heat of revolution.

"I can look people directly in the eye now, people from other countries," he told an American reporter, who was nearly as overcome as Machon. "We

are a free people again. We are part of Europe again." A big man with a thick mustache, he showed no embarrassment at the tears trickling down his face. It was the students who first rose up, and Machon has three in his family. "I am so thankful to my children for setting us free," he said. "And I am so happy that they can now live their lives in freedom."

The crowd was listening to Vaclav Havel, speaking from a balcony over the lovely wide boulevard of art nouveau elegance that, in a past era, was a spiritual heart of Europe. Havel, jailed, muzzled, reviled, had hammered away at his theme: the communist state was immoral, illogical, and inhuman. Though Czechoslovakia's best-known playwright, no one at home had seen his work on stage since Soviet tanks silenced the Prague Spring of 1968. But, in the end, Havel brought down the house.

Machon tried to describe what he felt. He heard the words coming out—freedom and democracy— and they did not satisfy him. As a geophysicist, he explained, he traveled to conferences in the West and found himself feeling half a man. He knew what his nation was and what someday it could be again. This was that day. "It is a wonderful day, wonderful," he said. "How can I say it?" Instead of trying further, he hugged the reporter and wept again.

That was revolution in Eastern Europe. There were the grand themes. An iron curtain rusted and flaked away. A political order was overturned, and an economic system collapsed. Nikita Khrushchev's shoe-banging on a table at the United Nations was a muffled echo in the past. But for all the sweeping ideology, the cold war clichés, the terrifying and tender symbols, this was a close-up revolution. It was the sum of personal victories. After four decades people found their dignity and reaffirmed their values. This was a triumph of human spirit.

Power came from faceless crowds, the huge masses that finally were too big to bully. But each individual in every crowd knew what was at risk: a job,

the few privileges wheedled from the system—or a life. Beyond the noise of chants and gunfire, there was a lilting leitmotiv. Hummed, strummed, sung out loud in a half-dozen languages, it was the same haunting melody of the American civil rights era, "We Shall Overcome."

In groups, individuals overcame, and they found again a national pride that was smothered by two generations of outside occupation.

Havel spoke not only for his own people in his presidential message on New Year's Day, 1990: "Everywhere in the world, people were surprised how these malleable, humiliated, cynical citizens of Czechoslovakia, who seemingly believed in nothing, found the tremendous strength within a few weeks to cast off the totalitarian system, in an entirely peaceful and dignified manner."

Havel raised two crucial questions: "Where did young people who had never known another system get their longing for truth, their love of freedom, their political imagination, their civic courage and civic responsibility? How did their parents, precisely the generation thought to have been lost, join them?"

In the heat of a revolution in Romania that was dignified if not peaceful, those same questions arose. On that Friday, December 22, when Nicolae Ceausescu fell, die-hard Securitate commandos tried to seize the television station. After midnight shells slammed into the thirteen-story building, and bullets shattered its windows. Marin Constantin, a producer of children's programs, took charge of the eighth floor. He doused the lights. When an overhead fixture would not turn off, he deftly smashed it with a chair. Gratiela Ripeanu and Elena Maria Ionescu, writers whose job had been cheerleading for Ceausescu, gaily shepherded visitors and colleagues to cover.

Throughout a terrifying siege, the little band joked about their plight while they privately exulted at their triumph. As dawn approached, they taught several foreign reporters an anthem from a past moment of glory, a song not heard in public since their parents were children: "Awake, Romania, from the mortal sleep into which you have been lulled by the evil tyrants."

For the next week, in the rubble of Bucharest, awakened Romanians seized passing journalists by the arm. Toma Cornelia seized mine. "You tell the world that we are not what people think we are," he said. "You tell them what we have done here." He had a sister who had moved to Loveland, Colorado. She could take no more of Nicolae Ceausescu. "You tell her we are starting a new life," Cornelia said. "Tell her we are waiting for her."

But he had the look I had just seen on the face of Zdenek Machon in Prague. It was a look that reporters came to recognize in all the revolutions, the tormented tableau of pride and pain fighting for the same space. Beneath joy and fervor, there was a chill of fear. Hardly anyone had any illusions about the future. Big Brother was going, but he was leaving a hell of a mess behind. And in case the repentant family missed him, he was not far away.

The notion of struggle, so beloved to Marxist-Leninists, was about to become hard reality. Struggling was what one was supposed to do against capitalists and imperialists who put self above society. In real life, people knew their enemy as an alien apparatus called the state. But in a system freed of choice, they endured or eluded. Some risked and suffered. Against a seamless monolith, however, few struggled. Lines were long, but there were basic necessities at the end. If not many thrived, no one starved. It was an old bargain: people pretended to work; the state pretended to pay them. Life went on without the intrusion of election campaigns or storms in the stock market.

Revolutions brought back the possibility to choose, but East Europeans made few choices. As one analyst put it, they had broken the eggs but still had to make the omelette. Interim governments scheduled elections for people whose democratic traditions had been stifled since the 1930s. Economists shaped a free market for societies without capital or credit. Anything was possible, including calamity.

Poland was as much a source of concern as of inspiration. The Solidarity labor movement kindled hope in 1980 with a courageous strike for better wages at the Lenin Shipyard. After a decade of battle—a struggle by any definition—Solidarity named a government to reshape Poland's economy. And early in 1990, at the shipyard in Gdansk where it all began, a worker's average salary was a banana and a half an hour.

The Poles' rough-and-tumble economic reform had a simple point of departure. They would let market forces wreak havoc and then pick up the pieces. The zloty was dashed on the rocks unmercifully. In October 1989 it was valued at 1,800 to the U.S. dollar. But people who wanted a real dollar paid 6,000 zlotys on the black market. In January banks gave a better rate than the black marketeers, 9,500 zlotys. Poland had a convertible currency. Poles could buy foreign currency with zlotys, but anyone with a fixed income, or a life's savings stashed in a mattress, teetered at the edge of ruin.

Subsidies ended, and prices mushroomed out of all logic. One day it cost four times as much to use a public telephone, though it was still five calls for a penny. But fuel also quadrupled. Poles shivered at home and left their cars on the street. Only wages remained controlled. Meat was suddenly plentiful, but housewives could not afford it. Families did without bread. Bananas, a traditional barometer of well-being, were abundant. But a banana cost a quarter, and workers made forty cents an hour.

Waiting for promises to materialize, Poles knew they needed much more outside help than was coming. They could not pay even interest on a $40-billion Western debt. Despite a first rush of Western warmth—"Let Poland be Poland," Ronald Reagan had once said, without elaboration—Poles realized the free market did not operate on sympathy, or justice. An old elite held positions of economic power.

Some people were getting much richer than others. Many got laid off. Poland's endemic stoicism took on a tinge of envy. Its trappings of capitalism included car thefts, beggars, and soup kitchens.

But, on a January morning, I went back to the Gdansk shipyard to ask workers what they thought of revolution. Roman Nurek, thirty-five, told me he was terrified that he might not be able to support his wife and infant daughter. Life, he said, was a struggle. I asked if the revolution was worth it. He looked at me like I was crazy.

Almost any date serves as the starting point of revolution. East Germans resisted in 1953. Hungarians rose from below in 1956. Czechoslovaks sought change from the top in 1968. Memories of those dates fired spirits in 1989. And a spark that began smoldering in 1970, at the shipyard in Gdansk, was never extinguished.

Gdansk, a Baltic seaport of Gothic glory caught between Poland and Germany for much of its history, has a soul of its own. Under a dramatic skyline of giant blue cranes, its 320-acre shipyard is a rust-flecked museum to socialist central planning. Workers rose up in 1970, in food riots, and troops cut them down with gunfire. No one forgot the scores of victims, but it took a decade for someone to fan the embers to flame.

In a revolution of unlikely leaders, Lech Walesa was among the least likely. He was a shipyard electrician, a workaday father with a peasant cunning. Laying out homespun social theory, he sounds more like Jerzy Kosinski's Chance Gardiner than Rousseau or Jefferson. More than one pilgrim to Gdansk found him abusively opinionated, often rude. He was something much bigger, however, a man who seized his time and bulled forward against all odds.

He organized workers into an independent labor union, Solidarity. Authorities fired him as a troublemaker. But Walesa's leap over the shipyard gate in 1980 has already gone down in history. He demanded the right to strike and, in the months that followed, established Solidarity as an independent movement.

In December 1981 Gen. Wojciech Jaruzelski brought out the tanks and declared martial law. He wanted to crush Solidarity and the ferment it stirred. Instead, he created martyrs, focused hatred, and triggered a process that no one again could control.

Though a labor movement, support for Solidarity crept into every segment of society. But, setting an example not always followed elsewhere in Eastern Europe, the Roman Catholic church took up the cudgel. In 1983, I stopped at a village church on the way to Krakow. People who could not get in the door filled the yard out front, praying on their own. Afterward, the priest told me which side God was on. He loosened his cassock to reveal the distinctive red Solidarnösc button pinned to his undershirt.

Elsewhere, Communist leaders sought to stay ahead of the curve. In Hungary Janos Kadar liberalized, experimenting with a small private sector and opening borders enough to give Hungarians a taste for life beyond the bloc. In East Germany and Bulgaria, hard-line central committees stood firm, attempting instead to supply their subjugated populations with the wherewithal of a reasonably comfortable life without options. Czechoslovak leaders tried to do the same, but too many bubbles boiled up from below.

Three years before Solidarity defied the system, a group of Czechoslovak intellectuals drafted a magna carta called Charter 77. A permanent roster of dissidents alternated as spokesmen. Other supporters made their positions known and accepted the consequences. One was Jiri Dienstbier, once a radio journalist and foreign correspondent who was jailed with Havel for antisocial behavior. Dienstbier went to work stoking coal in a factory until the 1989 revolution gave him a new job, minister of foreign affairs.

During the 1980s Czechoslovak authorities tried to keep up the pressure. They found Stalin's rulebook was no match for short-wave radio and manuscripts published abroad that were circulated hand to hand. Secret police could take notes. But what could they do about clusters of young people taking the air on the lovely old Charles Bridge, singing mournful spirituals from the days of slavery in America?

Sparks of defiance kept spirits alive. After the death of John Lennon, young Prague rockers painted tributes to the slain ex-Beatle on a wall under the Charles Bridge. By night, someone would scrawl, "You have your Lenin, Give us our Lennon," or "Give peace a chance." By day, police slapped on fresh white paint. Finally guards were posted. But every year, the rockers came back.

By 1985 the stage was set for Mikhail Gorbachev, the least likely revolutionary leader of them all. The common thread of all Eastern European revolutions was their eventual target: the Soviet Union. Creaking old Communist central committees were underpinned from Moscow. A Council of Mutual

Economic Assistance, or Comecon, was a Soviet pipe dream. But the Warsaw Pact, tipped with Soviet steel, was hard reality. If someone threatened to break loose, the Kremlin's tanks unleveled the playing field.

This time the Soviet Union sent no tanks. Gorbachev let events take their course within the context of two Russian words he had taught the West: *glasnost* and *perestroika.* The first conveyed transparency, the sort of openness not seen among the Russians and the peoples they dominate since the czar was overthrown in 1917. The second meant restructuring, a weeding out of seized-up systems and bankrupt values.

Serious analysts avoid reading the present in Eastern Europe and the Soviet Union, let alone the future. Historians eventually must determine whether Gorbachev had a choice—and what his bold venture meant to the end of the twentieth century. But enough of the past is clear. Gorbachev's temperance encouraged revolutionaries to defy him. His courage pushed hard-line Communist leaders to step aside. Whatever his motives, and whatever might happen next, Gorbachev changed the world.

When blood splashed the last falling domino in the Soviet bloc, Gorbachev even offered help to the revolutionaries. But they did not want it. For years many in the West had held up Nicolae Ceausescu as a sort of enlightened socialist, a bold maverick who refused orders from Soviet totalitarians. Romanians knew better. They loathed the madman who had led them into misery and pain over twenty-four years, and they would blot him out with their own hands.

Few dissidents had survived Ceausescu's paranoia. When the time came, however, heroes sprang up everywhere. Stirrings started in the town of Timisoara, when crowds of young people joined hands to protect Laszlo Tokes, a preacher of Hungarian origin.

The Hungarian minority in western Romania was high on the long list of subjects that nettled Ceausescu. Borders are always of fresh and serious concern in the Balkans. Romania lost the northern half of Moldavia to the Soviets after World War II, but it resumed its disputed possession of northern Transylvania, along with that region's population of unhappy Hungarians. Ceausescu had problems enough enforcing loyalty among Romanians who hated him as a tyrant. Transylvanians also hated him as a usurper.

As a dissident, Tokes was subtle and prudent. But in Ceausescu's Romania, every typewriter was registered with the secret police. Soon enough, the pastor was ordered to leave Timisoara. When officers went to get him, students shielded him with a human chain. A small rally grew to a peaceable demonstration. As tension mounted, Ceausescu explained his philosophy to his commanders: "You do not silence enemies by talking to them like a priest. You burn them." Troops opened fire on the youthful crowd. To the disbelief of elders long since inured to defeat, the crowd came back.

On Wednesday, December 20, Ceausescu returned from a trip to Iran and the next day summoned the masses for a spontaneous display of support. It was an act of unbelievable arrogance. And blindness. He harangued Romanians from his favorite balcony, at the Central Committee building overlooking Palace Square. Timisoara was the work of hooligans, foreign agitators. He would bolster student allowances and raise the minimum wage by a few more dollars a month. Up front, a claque of goons cheered on cue. In the back his beloved Romanians shuffled their feet in sullen silence.

Suddenly voices chanted, "Rat, rat," and "Death." Then most of the crowd picked up a steady chant: "Ceausescu *Dictatorul*" — Ceausescu Dictator. The immortal Conductor paused, a look of stricken surprise lingering on his face. He stepped back a moment, and the state-run television station cut to music. Propelled by the sharp jab from his wife and co-dictator, Elena, he returned to the microphone. It was too late. The balance of fear had shifted. For Romania, the last of the dominoes, it was all over but the bloodshed.

That night, students who had jeered Ceausescu gathered nearby at University Square. Some spoke out. Others quietly fell dead in the street. Ceausescu's secret police force was, in fact, an army of chilling efficiency in a place where nothing else worked. At its core, an elite band of sharpshooters followed their leader with blind detachment. From vantage points over the square, with sniperscopes and silencers, they systematically murdered students. When it was over, street crews hauled off the bodies and washed away the blood.

Friday morning, December 22, Bucharest was ready for another day in socialist paradise. Ceausescu went to work as usual. But young Romanians, in ragtag little groups that added up into the thousands, marched downtown to speak their minds. Tanks were sent out to meet them. In doorways people stood outside and hoped for the best. "Suddenly, I heard gunfire and thought, 'Oh, my God, they're killing them again,'" an American diplomat remembered later.

The gunfire, aimed into the air, was an announcement of surrender. Army commanders had had enough of Ceausescu; troops were joining the students. Tanks were swarmed by jubilant revolutionaries who jammed Christmas trees down their deadly barrels. Then everyone, rebels and defenders alike, went to call on the Ceausescus. By then, the dictator had caught on. From Palace Square, triumphant crowds watched the hated first couple take their brief helicopter ride into history.

That morning I followed the tumble of events on a teleprinter in Paris. By midnight I was on the streets of Bucharest, meeting hero after hero. At the first roadblock, Alex Florescu stopped a trio of American reporters and frisked them. He was a mild-mannered young man who, until that evening, had worked in a hospital and averted his eyes in the suspected presence of secret police. "I'll help you," he said, "but first I want to drop this off at my house." He nodded toward a yellow sports bag, which, he explained, was full of Molotov cocktails.

We had arrived on a small charter flight. The airport was dark, and gunfire echoed in the distance.

We had no visas. A burly border guard approached and, with a sunny smile, said: "Welcome to Romania." At immigration I greeted the agent, "How are you?" He grinned. "Much better. Now." The customs woman merely gave me a cheery wave. A bus appeared to take people into town, but mysteriously, it would not leave. Finally, we saw why: a hostess had gone off to find the new laissez-passer, a huge Romanian flag with the Communists' emblem ripped out of the middle.

Insurgents made barricades of trucks and fallen trees, even pastry carts wheeled out of a bakery, and twelve-year-olds armed with sticks helped to man them. We flagged down a man who drove us into town in his little sedan. I asked what was happening. "Oh," he said, "just a small revolution in a small place."

At the television station, the seat of power in those first crucial days, tension was electric. When Ceausescu left, the Committee for National Salvation locked itself in Studio Four and shaped a new Romania, ad hoc and on the air.

Ceausescu had left behind his secret guard, the Securitate, in a desperate plan to sow chaos. They melted away only to reappear again in a network of safe houses and tunnels equipped for long-term survival. Snipers dropped victims with a single shot to the head and then vanished while terrorized army troops blasted away their ammunition at an empty apartment. If the Securitate rescued Ceausescu, it would be civil war. But the new government was safe so long as its comforting image remained on television screens across Romania.

We installed ourselves on the eighth floor, near a telephone and a telex, to await developments. For a while it looked like the resistance had melted away. Then, a few minutes after 2 A.M., the neighborhood was suddenly Bunker Hill.

Securitate gunfire slammed into the thirteen-story building. Troops inside replied with a withering barrage. None of the defending soldiers had fired more than a handful of rounds in their lives—and never at anything that shot back. People went up and down in elevators, a high risk in a building under siege. When I pointed this out, I found out why. Someone had tried to use the stairs and was shot by a nervous soldier.

At first the screen flickered, but Free Romanian Television stayed on the air. It broadcast an appeal for help. Within minutes, we could see from the eighth floor, nameless heroes appeared on the square below.

The gesture, beyond brave, bordered on crazy. They had formed a human shield between the studio and Securitate positions in the upper floors of nearby buildings. Three thousand people assembled on the square below, scattering only when gunfire dropped down toward the lower floors.

It was only later, at the cemetery with grieving families, that I realized what I was watching. Nicisor Paunoiu, an elevator mechanic with two kids, stormed a Securitate position unarmed with three friends. He was cut down by automatic fire. Dan Adrian Urucu, a student on the square, was shot in the back. Victim after victim died defending the television and radio stations.

In the early hours of Saturday, Petre Roman came out of Studio Four to fill us in. He was no one special in Ceausescu's Romania, a professor of fluid mechanics at the Polytechnic Institute who kept head down and mouth shut. Roman had contacts with a few like-minded men and women, and some mysterious plotting had been done. Mainly, he was there on the street when the tank crews rallied to the people. He announced the popular uprising before the television cameras and then joined others to penetrate the Central Committee building and persuade top military commanders to give up the ghost.

That night under siege, he was just another face-less hero in a field jacket, not especially articulate and unsure of where the whole adventure was headed. The next time I saw him, he was in an immaculately cut double-breasted suit and a silk tie, smooth as a network talk-show host, explaining on prime-time French television what the government he headed planned to do with freedom and democracy.

In Romania, as in Czechoslovakia, there were those words again. Young people tried them out, speaking them aloud. At the Bucharest Emergency Hospital, medical students clustered around me and, prompted by questions, probed at the words, freedom and de-mocracy, as if they were dissecting exotic birds.

"What is it to live free, to travel free, to speak freely?" mused Ioana Popescu, "We have only seen dark and silence." A friend, Anda Preda, added, "We can't realize what freedom is. You grew up in free-dom, and you do not realize what this means to us." She paused and apologized: "I've learned English eleven years, and this the first time I speak it."

Bogdan Lazaroae, who ended up translating for reporters, was sometimes as confused as the outsiders. "I am afraid people will ask me what I am doing with foreigners, but no one asks," he said. "That's a little bit of freedom. I am afraid to speak the name of Ceausescu in the street, maybe someone will tell me I'm an enemy, but they don't. That's a little bit of freedom."

The student doctors also had to define Christ-mas. This was December 24 and, for the first time in forty-three years, carols were played in public. "May-be you can't understand what Christmas this year means for us," said Anda Preda. "You hear these Christ-mas songs every year, and you are used to them."

Ioana Popescu started to speak of family and joy but kept glancing up the corridor at men her own age bleeding from gunshot wounds. "Next year, we will have Christmas and freedom and know what they mean," she said. "Next year we will have Christmas."

The words were more tangible up the hill at the Metropolitan Cathedral. As Christmas approached, Romanians had come to thank God and their chil-dren for deliverance. One was a kindly mother named Victoria Ionita. She told a translator she was "very happy," but her eyes suggested that was a feeble un-derstatement. "There were so many years when I did not come to church for fear of the government," she said. "Now there is shooting in the streets, but I come because of trust in God."

On the open cathedral porch, heat from so many thin yellow candles warmed the icy air. In silent knots, people waited in line to speak to three American reporters. It was as if we were at once their confessors and their conduit to a world they had just rejoined. Every eye was swollen and red. I noticed one man whose face strained to hold its composure. His features twitched and stiffened until he suddenly burst into uncontrollable sobs. Twenty years of guilt, shame, and suppressed anger let loose all at once. Like me, he was a journalist.

"All the things that I have seen and stood by silently for so many years," he began. "They have killed children, thousands." He spilled out memories of Ceausescu's atrocities. Coolly he described a process of censorship and mind control that might have shaken Orwell. Then he broke down again, repeating to me but mostly to himself, "I'm so sorry. I'm so happy."

For East Germans, who arose before the Czechoslovaks and Romanians, neither freedom nor democracy needed any definition. Night after night, they sat behind their ugly gray wall and watched both of those concepts flourish next door. By the fall of 1989, fresh winds blew over the closed borders, and spirits lifted.

People spilled onto the streets of Leipzig to tell their aged, atrophied leaders what they thought. And, miraculously, East Germans began to get away.

Among the most enduring images of Cold War Communism was the East German border guard, with his dogs and death rays, ready to impose instant capital punishment on anyone trying to flee. Even with papers in order, no one could cross from East to West without a spasm of chill at the hard stare of the guards, the elaborate clanking gates, the electronic sensors, and the no-man's-land kept clear as a field of fire. Usually only the old or the privileged made it through the gates, and still it was never easy.

In Berlin there was the wall, festooned with enough barbed wire to circle the globe. It went up in 1961, bisecting the old capital of Mitteleuropa. Potsdamer Platz, once the busiest crossroads on the continent, became the back door of the world's largest prison. Over the years eighty people were shot to death trying to flee over the wall. The rest of the country was sealed off just as tightly. But East Germans could visit their fraternal allies around the bloc—the Hungarians, for instance.

On May 2 Hungarian guards snipped away a hundred yards of the iron curtain along the border with Austria. Hungary, which gave passports to its own citizens, itched to rejoin Europe. Breaching the barrier was a gesture, and it had the same effect as piercing a small hole in the hull of a large ship. By the end of August, thousands of Germans had found their way through.

Then obliging Czechoslovak authorities began looking the other way. East Germans besieged West German missions in Prague and Warsaw. After bitter negotiation, East German authorities let them go; their special trains only had to pass through East Germany on the way for a touch of feigned regularity. Pretense was preserved to the last.

Into the fall, endless lines of overheated little sedans streamed out via Czechoslovakia. But people were fleeing, not traveling. For those with families and deep attachments, that was a major difference.

For two years a regular Monday night "prayer for peace" at Saint Nicolas Church in Leipzig had attracted young people anxious for change. During 1989 the crowds increased, and the message grew more pointed. Encouraged by the emigration, churchgoers braved riot police to gather in the streets. By November the Monday night rallies in Leipzig had swelled to three hundred thousand people. The writing was all over the wall.

In the face of all odds, an opposition crystallized around a painter and Joan of Arc figure named Baerbel Bohley and a microbiologist, Jens Reich, whose career was sidetracked by his political enthusiasms. Their New Forum fired imagination and pumped up courage. The huge Leipzig crowds roared: "Take down the wall, we need bricks." Finally, on November 4 in East Berlin, a half-million Germans came out of their homes. Stefan Heym, like Havel a writer who had kept at his message, thundered: "We have emerged from our silence, and we are learning to walk, heads high, after bowing before the kaiser, the Nazis, and what came later."

The Berlin rally whistled down Guenter Schabowski, the reformist Communist official in charge of the capital. On November 9, however, Schabowski had the stage all to himself at a press conference. He described his movement. Forty-five minutes into the briefing, someone asked about travel restrictions. What about the wall? Well, he told reporters, that's why we freed travel *"ab sofort"* (immediately). Reporters shouted: What? Schabowski read quickly through a paper in his hand and repeated: *"Ab sofort."* At the AP Berlin bureau, Nesha Starcevic was watching on television. "They're opening the borders!" he screamed, and he flashed the news around the world.

It was that simple, just like one of the uncounted champagne bottles that opened over the following week. Slow, steady twisting loosened the cork. And the expanding pressure inside suddenly escaped in a pop the world would never forget.

When Schabowski spoke, it was dinnertime in Berlin. The news did not sink in, and in any case the declaration was vague about whether people first had to check out with the police. At 10 P.M., the Brandenburg Gate was all but deserted. Then it was time for "Tagesthemen," West Berlin television's equivalent of "Nightline," the newscast that for years told East Berliners things about their lives they never heard at home. People were coming across in some places, Tagesthemen reported. Checkpoint Charlie might open soon.

Alison Smale of AP raced to the checkpoint, arriving with the first few East Germans. Within minutes there were three hundred more. Border guards were friendly but firm: no new orders. They opened an outer gate, sending electricity through the anxious crowd. But no one knew what to do next. Finally a man in charge persuaded almost everyone to return in the morning. Angelika Wachs was not going back. She had a visa to leave the following week and saw no reason to wait. At a few minutes to midnight, the gate opened to let Smale return to West Berlin, as her one-day visa demanded. Wachs slipped through with her. The guard shrugged and stamped both passports.

The two women, both thirty-four and crazed with glee, were the first to get through Checkpoint Charlie. Only a few hundred West Berliners were there to cheer the historic breakthrough. Angelika Wachs looked around and observed, "It's really quite normal." Then she went off to sample freedom.

Within a few hours, nothing about Berlin was normal. East Germans probed the city in their funny little Trabants, gawking at the forbidden fruit down every brightly lit street. Soon there was too much traffic for anyone to move. Few people minded. The revelry was on foot. People danced and sang or just threw back their heads and shouted at the top of their lungs.

More than one hundred thousand came over immediately, and others would keep on coming. Everywhere there were scenes of personal triumph. David Turnley watched two women fall upon each other with sobs of joy. Putting aside his camera, he asked them how they were related. They were not, one explained. For twenty years they had waved to one another from apartment windows on either side of the wall. Until that moment they had never met.

Alison Smale's night went on and on. She found

an old couple who remembered the western part of the city from when it was named, simply, Berlin. The couple explored old haunts in a taxi, dazzled, bewildered, and hovering at the edge of tears. Finally the woman's gaze settled on an open shop. "Imagine," she said. "Fresh flowers at this hour." Then she broke down and wept.

In Hungary I tried to draw people out on how it felt to be free. Answers were somehow forced, even hollow. Though pioneers at revolution, Hungarians had no real catharsis. No single moment in time marked the turning point. One of the proud little nation's principal revolutionary heroes, ironically enough, was a Communist member of the Politburo, Imre Pozsgay, who insisted on the rights of opposition parties. Even before angry crowds had collected elsewhere in Eastern Europe, the Communist Party quietly dropped out of the communism business.

Foreign Minister Gyula Horn finally tore open the curtain. All night on August 22, he pondered what to do about German refugees. Hungary wanted to let them go, but a 1968 treaty required Berlin's approval. Finally he decided: the treaty violated human rights.

But for many Hungarians the popular perception of their revolution—that it was somehow given to them without a fight—has a bitter tinge. They were the ones who first tasted Soviet steel. For three decades they resisted the deadening overlay of outside ideology, pushing it back bit by bit. No one listening around a café table at the old New York or sitting on a log by the campfire at a midnight party on the outskirts of Budapest would have considered Hungarians bystanders to their fate.

Like the Hungarians, the Poles can identify no moment of revolution. There was Walesa's first act of defiance. A string of victories was studded with setbacks, almost as if to give flesh to the Poles' beloved watchword for the world in general: "Life is brutal and full of *zasadkas*." A *zasadka* is a booby trap, a sudden obstacle thrown in the path of a suffering people who manage to thrive, whatever the *zasadkas*.

Poles tend to look down at their fingers when Americans characterize their revolution, Eastern Europe's revolution, as a simple victory over capitalism, proof that "our" system is better than "their" system. There is something to that. But no one rose up over a toaster or a trip to Disneyland.

In Poland it was a war of attrition against the daily compromises that reduce your soul. You win it merely by fighting it. Adam Michnik of Solidarity explained it in a letter from prison: "You score a victory not when you win power but when you remain faithful to yourself."

A Polish friend of mine brought this home on a trip to Gdansk when he spent a day interpreting my questions about freedom. The answers were broad, focusing on the humiliating, dehumanizing process of an alien ideology imposed from without. Because it was there did not mean it was there to stay. Finally, exasperated at my denseness, he explained why no one addressed the point of sudden freedom: "We have always been free."

Bulgaria's quiet little revolution was as startling as the more tumultuous ones farther north. Of all the European states once regarded as Soviet satellites, Bulgaria was the only one that seemed to be in a natural orbit. Historical and religious ties linked Bulgaria to Mother Russia—in the last century Russians joined Bulgarians against the Turks—and it took few artificial contortions to link their economies.

Fired by the same zeal as their neighbors, emboldened by the same forces, Bulgarians let their leaders know what they thought. Their stalwart old warden, Todor Zhivkov, was bundled out of office and jailed in November 1989 after three decades at the top. The ubiquitous secret police were tamed. The senior cabinet ministers who rose against Zhivkov's corrupt despotism steered Bulgaria toward reform. Freer expression and political options were on the way.

If the cornerstone in the Balkans broke away, could the Baltic states last much longer? In 1990, Lithuania went to the brink. Estonia and Latvia, seized by Stalin at the same ignoble moment in history, would not be far behind. No one could guess. But, it was clear enough, Europe had not seen an end to revolutions.

In fact, as the 1990s began, it seemed as if the first moments of revolution were only a prelude. Disturbing evidence raised fears about the reflexes of people brought up under tyranny and economic fantasy. A thirst for revenge, for a sudden reversal of fortunes, sometimes overshadowed urgent business at hand. At the extreme, National Salvation Front, which led Romania to freedom, found itself in open warfare with other parties even before elections could be organized. Heroes of the uprising resigned from the front's Central Committee, denouncing its "Stalinist tactics."

Even in Hungary, where discord was gentlemanly, there was more democracy than some people wanted. Fifty political parties organized to contest spring elections. The result was a paralysis that kept former Communist managers and officials in control of a large portion of the nation's vital forces.

Walesa, who fought so hard to bring democracy to Poland, lobbied furiously to put it off for a while. A government with a popular mandate must be free to decree a set of laws to allow the country to function in the free market, he argued. "We are like a car with four wheels all going in different directions," he told me early in 1990. "We are going full speed and sliding backward."

Hope pervaded Czechoslovakia, and a spirit there encouraged others. For all the trauma in Romania, and despite the bitter long march in Poland, the Czechoslovaks' revolution stood as an enduring symbol. It was deadly serious business. But somehow pathos collided with absurdity to produce a chain of events the most whimsical of Bohemian minds could not have conjured up on paper. It was one place where people understood that words were as important as deeds.

It was a revolution born on a stage in a theater called the Magic Lantern. Havel, with his impish gleam and rumpled brown jeans, seemed as much an over-fifty Dennis the Menace as a candidate to be an Old World head of state. Jan Carnogursky went from prisoner to deputy prime minister, in charge of the secret police, with hardly a stop at home to pick up a toothbrush. And the Czechoslovaks loved it.

You could see it when Foreign Minister Jiri Dienstbier visited Warsaw at the start of 1990. These formal calls to fraternal capitals were once the province of somber old men bent on proving form was the key to power. But visitors and hosts could hardly keep a straight face for all the winking. After all, a former coal stoker and prisoner was representing Czechoslovakia before a government loyal to a former prisoner whose Gdansk office was decorated with a cartoon showing the once-powerful Jaruzelski carrying his briefcase.

Dienstbier was more of what you would expect from a people who used to throw medieval tyrants out of upper-story windows and who, more recently, all but worshipped a fat fictitious soldier, a novelist's character, given to sticking his finger in the eye of anyone in authority. At the outset, when outsiders were swept up in the grand themes, I drafted a paragraph that likened Czechoslovaks to captive-born lions learning how to roar. A local journalist friend glanced at it and muttered, "You mean koala bears." But for all the self-deprecation and humor, it was a very big moment.

In an advanced stage of uprising, a Czech photographer stopped a moment and approached David Turnley. Beaming, he spoke to his colleague in stilted English. "We have a tender—is that the right word?—revolution." David assured him it was.

It did not start out tender. Students massed on the streets of Prague at a time when police did everything they could to discourage them. They kept coming back. On a Friday night, November 17, police waded savagely into a youthful crowd, thrashing bare heads with heavy wood sticks and kicking their victims as they fell. Word flashed around Prague that young Martin Smid had been beaten to death.

By the time Smid denied the report in person, the balance of fear had shifted. Czechoslovakia had had enough. Students had started it, but their parents and grandparents arose to join them. Against the possibility of massive retaliation, they fought their revolution with key rings held aloft to jingle in ominous protest. As ammunition, they used candle wax.

A thick pool of wax coated every trace of blood on the streets of Prague. Impromptu shrines, tended day and night, lighted the spots where students fell injured. Flowers and photographs commemorated each encounter. Suddenly, in honor of a 1969 martyr never forgotten, there was a massive circle of fire at the foot of the towering statue to Vaclav, the good king Wenceslas. A student named Jan Palach had immolated himself there to protest the Soviet invasion. Later, Havel was put in prison for placing flowers on the site. Now Palach, along with Vaclav Havel and the old hero-king, would stir a nation.

Day after day crowds ignored arctic weather to carpet the 800-yard-long Champs-Elysées known as Wenceslas Square. They packed into Sparta Stadium. People chanted, *"Svobodne Volby!"* (Free elections) and *"Demisi!"* (Resign). They heard Communist leaders make tepid promises. They heard repentant security policemen, consumed with shame at their repression. And Czechoslovaks rallied around their symbols, new and old.

One morning a single photographer waited as a stooped and aging man stepped off the bus from Bratislava. He carried a cheap briefcase and a hat tucked under his arm. When the photographer went to work, the man asked if he could be left in peace. It was his first return to Prague since he had been cashiered to a minor job in the forestry service for daring to flirt with reform in 1968. A few hours later, the gray old man was smiling, speaking to a half-million people chanting, "Dubcek! Dubcek!"

The real test came on Monday, November 27. Civic Forum, the umbrella organization that comprised students, intellectuals, and a range of dissidents, called for a brief general strike. It was a terrific gamble. If workers responded, the point would be made. If not, however, Communist authorities could crush the opposition with vigor.

At noon on Monday, to a joyous cacophony of sirens, bus horns, and bells, the nation came to a halt. Within ten days, non-Communists and converted Communists steered Czechoslovakia toward free elections and an open economy.

Outside Czechoslovakia, much of the world expected to see Alexander Dubcek back in power. That appealed to a broad sense of logic and cosmic order, a completion of the unfinished symphony. But the Czechoslovaks' drumbeat, muffled toward understatement and always with its own particular rhythm, was into a new age. Many were done with the past and those linked to its politics.

Czechoslovakia preferred a writer-thinker in the tradition of their beloved Tomas Garrigue Masaryk, the philosopher who led an uprising that took them out of the Austro-Hungarian empire early in the century. Statues of Masaryk always show him ramrod stiff, serious in a long black coat, and people still wanted a man who could open the opera in a tuxedo. But they needed someone who could also come to work in a rumpled lavender shirt and talk about Captain Beefheart with Frank Zappa.

Havel's appeal was not his magnetism. It was that he understood and gave voice to everyone's thoughts. "We have become morally ill because we have become accustomed to saying one thing and thinking another," he told his people. "None of us is merely a victim of it, because all of us helped to create it."

In the end it was those little moments of triumph, like Zdenek Machon's, that brought such glory to the Czechoslovaks' revolution. And the wonderful, literary irony. Both were everywhere. There was, for instance, Hradcany—Prague's Castle.

The president's office is in the Castle, a brooding medieval citadel on a bluff above old Prague, just over the Vltava River. That was where Havel directed a letter to President Gustav Husak in 1975, a courageous petition for change. From inside the Castle, Husak kept things dark and gray, in lockstep with the Kremlin. Outside, Czechoslovaks and tourists alike strolled past the closed doors and through the cobblestoned village inside the ramparts to a short lane of colorful, odd-angled, dollhouse-size dwellings. Franz Kafka had lived in one.

Passing the Kafka studio, most outsiders think of cockroaches. *The Metamorphosis* is the tormented novelist's best-known work. But Czechoslovaks often remember *The Castle*. It was about a man—a symbol; this was Kafka—who spent his life trying to enter a castle. The writer had trouble working out his fate. He chose an ending, but after his death someone found an optional version. One suggested hope; the other, futility.

There were grand universal themes to Czechoslovakia's tender revolution. But to the people who fought it, there were hidden depths of feelings brought on by such details as those posters that read HAVEL NA HRAD—Havel to the Castle.

(I have reported on Eastern Europe's revolutions for The Associated Press, my employer for twenty-five years. Although these observations are my own, I am grateful to my AP colleagues for graciousness and assistance. —M.R.)

FACING PAGE: PRAGUE—*With a joyous cacophony, Czechoslovaks declared revolution. Horns blared, sirens screamed. The message sounded from church spires, factory loudspeakers, and trolleys stalled in traffic. Many people simply held up their key rings and jingled them. Others banged loudly on bells.* (DT)

PAGES 40 AND 41: PRAGUE—*Foreshadowing events to come, a jubilant Mikhail Gorbachev enthusiastically presses flesh outside the Magic Lantern Theater in Prague. Three years later, Vaclav Havel directed a revolution from the theater's stage.* (PT)

PAGES 42 AND 43: EAST BERLIN—*East German troops march by Gorbachev during his October 1989 visit to celebrate the fortieth anniversary of the German Democratic Republic. Within days, his host, Erich Honecker, would fall in disgrace, and the Soviet satellite would be headed out of its orbit.* (PT)

SARBOGARD, Hungary—*The world trembled in 1956 when Soviet tanks rolled into Hungary. With more quiet relief than fanfare early in 1989, many of them rolled out again.* (DT)

SARBOGARD—*Comrades in arms say good-bye, headed to different parts of the Soviet Union. Most were as happy to leave as Hungarians were to see them go.* (DT)

FACING PAGE: SARBOGARD—*A Hungarian youngster inspects the Red Army rifle of a soldier earmarked by Mikhail Gorbachev for immediate departure.* (DT)

PAGE 48: LEIPZIG—*In the fateful fall of 1989, youthful Monday night marchers carried not only banners demanding relief from Communist rule but also photos of their unlikely ally, the chief Communist himself.* (DT)

PAGE 49: PRAGUE—*When Alexander Dubcek demanded "socialism with a human face" in 1968, Soviet tanks crushed the uprising. This time, uprising was revolution. Dubcek's "human face" was hoisted again over Czechoslovakia, and only socialism was in question.* (PT)

BUDAPEST—*At a refugee camp in Hungary, before the wall opened in November 1989, an East German girl waits for freedom. Her mother had been fired for political reasons, and the little family was headed West.* (PT)

FACING PAGE: EAST BERLIN—*Around the Gethsemane Church on a Sunday afternoon, a girl enlivens a gathering of protesters who sense a new wind wafting across their hated wall.* (DT)

PAGES 52 AND 53: EAST BERLIN—*In the smoke-hazed candlelit Bohemian loft of a Prenzlauer Berg building abandoned to squatters, East German students keep a vigil on their revolution.* (DT)

SOFIA—*Bulgarian teenagers, eye and fashion sense set on the West, watch for a chance to let their aging leaders know what they think about the future.* (DT)

FACING PAGE: VILNIUS, Lithuania—*At the far edge of Eastern Europe early in 1989, before the wave of revolution caught fire, a young girl fans the flame with a flag of Lithuania at an independence day rally.* (PT)

LEIPZIG—*Their rally ending, a New Forum crowd bursts into a rousing version of the anthem and leitmotiv of East European revolution, "We Shall Overcome."* (DT)

FACING PAGE: PRAGUE—*Out on the streets to protest the way police savagely beat student demonstrators, two young Czechoslovaks wrap themselves in a flag and deliver a silent message.* (PT)

FACING PAGE: VILNIUS, Lithuania—*While noisy protests reverberated through the streets, the devout took their struggle to church, including this aged Lithuanian woman at the central cathedral of Vilnius.* (PT)

PAGES 60 AND 61: EAST BERLIN—*In a country that thwarts dissent, a fledgling opposition must first find a place to meet. In Berlin this meeting place was inside and outside the Gethsemane Church, led by a pastor committed to the cause. An early October crowd demands the release of people arrested the night before.* (PT)

KRAKOW—*A Pole brings his painting of the Virgin to the Mariack church on Krakow's old square, the home parish of Pope John Paul II.* (DT)

GDANSK—*Lech Walesa prays at Saint Brygida's Church.* (DT)

PAGES 64 AND 65: BRASOV, Romania—*Women attend church in Brasov, sustaining their faith in the face of religious repression, six months before their grandchildren rise up in revolution.* (PT)

PAGES 66 AND 67: LVOV, Ukraine—*The priest of a banned church conducts services in secret at a project apartment building, keeping faith alive as revolution simmers below the surface.* (PT)

FACING PAGE: PRAGUE—*For many Eastern Europeans, revolution meant not only personal liberties but
also a revival of proud national spirits suppressed for four
decades. On Wenceslas Square, just before one of the rallies that would set them free, Czechoslovaks put out their
colors.* (PT)

PAGES 70 AND 71: VILNIUS, Lithuania—*At an
independence day rally in front of the cathedral, Lithua-
nians remind Moscow and the world beyond that they
have not forgotten who they are.* (PT)

PAGES 72 AND 73: PRAGUE—*At Wenceslas
Square, a worker asserts his new ability to stand up and
shout.* (DT)

PAGES 74 AND 75: SOFIA—*Irate Bulgarians wave
a list of demands at policemen outside the state-run television station. Citizens, promised freer speech, held new
leaders to their word.* (DT)

PAGES 76 AND 77: EAST BERLIN—*Demonstra-
tors take their cause into the streets of Berlin, a counter-
point to celebrations for the fortieth anniversary of East
Germany, celebrated on October 7, 1989.* (PT)

PAGES 78 AND 79: EAST BERLIN—*Riot police impose order on the Schoenhauserallee, near Gethsemane
Church, after a night of violent clashes. Gorbachev, in
town for the fortieth-anniversary celebrations, had just
gone home.* (PT)

GDANSK—*Walesa addresses a group of West Germans interested in investing in Poland.* (PT)

KATOWICE, Poland—*Coal miners prepare to climb into the elevator and head down to work.* (DT)

BUCHAREST—*Beside himself with fury and relief, a demonstrator jabbed twin victory signs at an unseen target and yelled, again and again, "Ceausescu Dictator."* (PT)

FACING PAGE: BUCHAREST—*At Belo Cemetery, after the revolution, stricken families bury their dead and vow that the deaths will have served a purpose.* (PT)

PAGES 84 AND 85: HUNGARY-AUSTRIA BORDER—*The iron curtain parted slowly at first, at a spot west of Budapest. In early September these two youths crouched in the grass waiting to join thousands who had already fled. They were stopped at gunpoint, twenty yards from a gap in the fence. One surrendered. The other took off like a deer, leaping and running, risking the fate of a man shot there ten days earlier. He made it. Two days later, East Germans poured across freely into Austria.* (PT)

HUNGARY-AUSTRIA BORDER—*When the border finally opened, East Germans broke out the champagne. One man's banner blotted out the initial letter D for "Democratic," added to his country's name long ago by Communist leaders whose idea of democracy left out the people.* (PT)

PAGES 88 AND 89: HUNGARY-AUSTRIA BORDER—*A brother and sister emerge from their car in Austria, free at last.* (PT)

PAGES 90 AND 91: BERLIN—*At the wall, where guards once spent hours scrutinizing travelers and thrusting mirrors under cars, an official uses a portable visa stamper for speed.* (DT)

BERLIN—*A lone guard patrols the Berlin wall, seen from West Berlin, with the Brandenburg Gate behind.* (DT)

PAGES 94 AND 95: BERLIN—*As the wall is pierced at Potsdamer Platz, once the busiest crossroads in Europe until the cold war sealed it shut, militiamen hold back Sunday crowds.* (PT)

FACING PAGE: PRAGUE — *The Czechoslovak revolution, a sudden popular uprising, quickly took its shape around a group calling itself the Civic Forum. Daily, at briefing time, reporters crammed into the Magic Lantern Theater to watch the scenario unfold. Sometimes Vaclav Havel, pensive or playful, gave a news conference.* (PT)

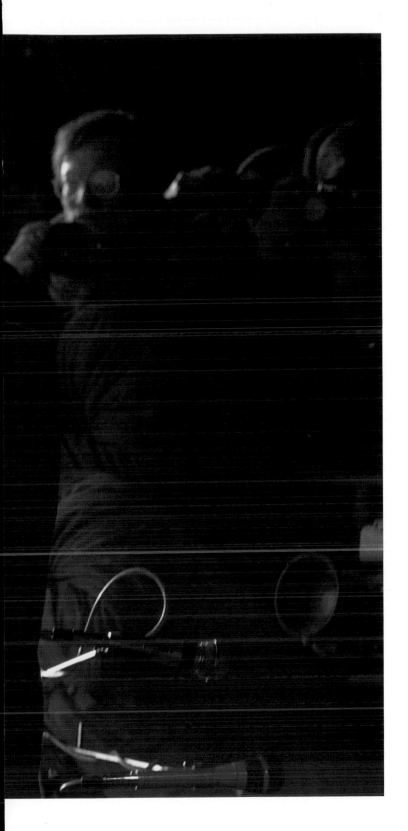

PRAGUE—*Alexander Dubcek, banished into obscurity after the 1968 "Prague Spring," returned on November 24, 1989.* (PT)

PAGES 108 AND 109, AND 110 AND 111: PRAGUE—*In Czechoslovakia the question was whether the workers would join in. They did. At the Praha auto parts plant, striking workers applaud the revolution.* (both, PT)

PRAGUE—*On the Sunday that Czechoslovaks stopped to think about what they had won, streets erupted in joy.* (DT)

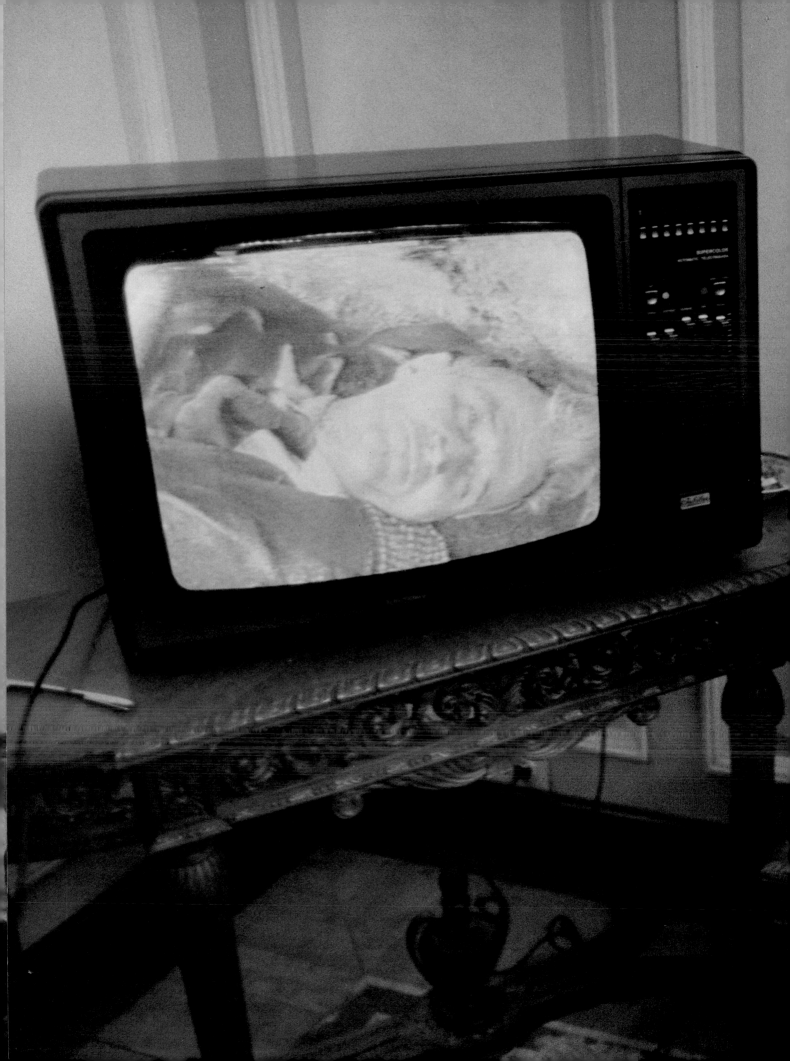

BUCHAREST—*A sudden sniper attack three days into the revolution sends Romanians diving for cover in Palace Square, outside the Central Committee building.* (DT)

BUCHAREST—*Passersby pause at what remains of a suspected Securitate terrorist, killed and burned in front of the television station.* (DT)

PAGES 132 AND 133: BUCHAREST—*Tanks stand guard outside the charred hulk of Bucharest's university library. Most of the contents, including priceless old manuscripts, were lost.* (PT)

PAGES 134 AND 135: BUCHAREST—*A soldier makes his way through debris in the university library, where hundreds of thousands of books and documents burned.* (DT)

BUCHAREST—*Romanian soldiers, who rallied to the
revolution, were honored with carnations.* (PT)

FACING PAGE: BUCHAREST—*A soldier patrols a
side street holding an AK-47 loaded with a flower.* (PT)

BUCHAREST—*In Romania's revolution, as in the others, there was joy and relief. But for Romanians, that was only the start of it. Avram Constantin watched as a truck piled with war dead drove past, on its way to Belo Cemetery.* (PT)

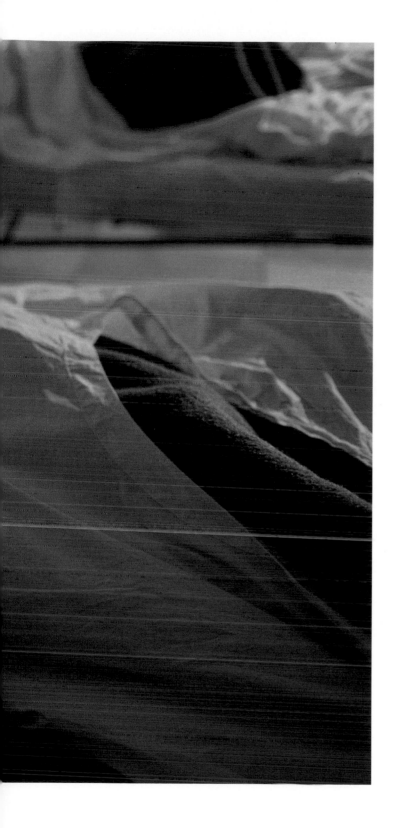

BUCHAREST—*A Securitate terrorist, still handcuffed to his bed at Bucharest Emergency Hospital, dies of his wounds.* (PT)

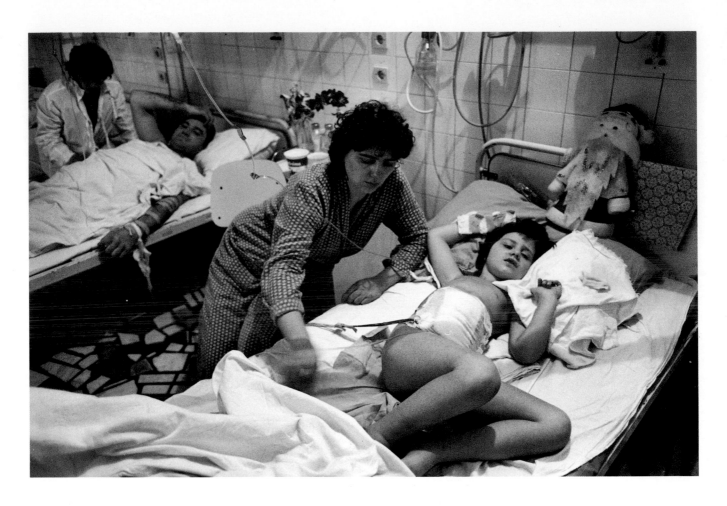

BUCHAREST—*At the emergency hospital, a mother comforts her daughter, victim of a Securitate sniper. A Santa Claus over the bed testifies that, with it all, it is Christmas.* (DT)

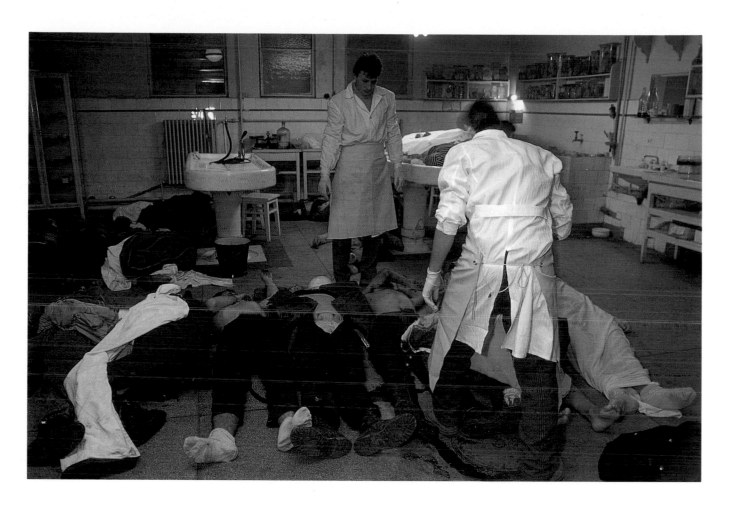

BUCHAREST—*A makeshift morgue fills quickly.* (PT)

PAGES 146 AND 147: BUCHAREST—*A victim lies in state at a small chapel reopened for the first time in years.* (PT)

PAGES 154 AND 155: BUCHAREST—*Candles honor the dead at Belo Cemetery.* (PT)

FACING PAGE: BUCHAREST—*Gunfire echoed across Romania on Christmas Day, but so did the first carols heard publicly in more than four decades. On a downtown street emptied by sniper fire, a woman happily enfolds a tree in her embrace.* (DT)

PAGES 158 AND 159: PRAGUE—*There was jubilation at the feet of Good King Wenceslas.* (DT)

PAGES 160 AND 161: PRAGUE—*Vaclav Havel and Alexander Dubcek toast the resignation of the Communist politburo.* (PT)

PAGES 162 AND 163: BERLIN—*East Germans in West Berlin sing, celebrating the end of the wall.* (DT)

BUDAPEST—*Seen from the Danube, along a promenade beloved to young couples, the revitalized Hungarian parliament is no longer a symbolic monument to the past.* (DT)

FACING PAGE: BUCHAREST—*A young couple, soldiers, wear the white armband that identifies them as insurgents.* (PT)

BUCHAREST—*Throughout the brief revolution, civilians brought food to the troops. A woman pours hot coffee in Palace Square.* (PT)

BUCHAREST—*Mao said power grows out of the barrel*
of a gun. But order comes from a new broom. (DT)

BUCHAREST—*A grateful hug for a soldier at Palace Square.* (DT)

PAGES 170 AND 171: BUCHAREST—*A commandeered truck takes reveling revolutionaries through the streets.* (DT)

PAGES 172 AND 173: PRAGUE—*Joy on a public bus at the beginning of Wenceslas Square.* (DT)

VILNIUS, Lithuania—*Red Army troops, once feared in Soviet Lithuania, struggle to hold back a crowd storming Communist Party headquarters.* (PT)

PAGES 176 AND 177: TBLISI, Georgia—*As ripples of revolution were felt in the Soviet republics, Georgians took to the streets. In 1990 militiamen hem in a crowd commemorating the April 9, 1989, massacre of twenty Georgians by Soviet troops silencing a protest.* (PT)

PAGES 178 AND 179: SOFIA—*And Bulgarians, like other Eastern Europeans, await the future.* (DT)

Bucharest, Romania, 1989. (DT)

Tblisi, Georgia, 1990. (PT)

Acknowledgments and Photo Credits

David Turnley

Back cover, 2–3, 4–5, 6–7, 8–9, 38, 44–45,
46, 47, 48, 51, 52–53, 55, 56, 62, 63, 72–73,
74–75 courtesy National Geographic
Society, 81, 90–91, 92–93, 97, 98–99,
100–101, 102, 113, 116–117, 118–119,
122–123, 128–129, 130, 131, 134–135, 144,
152–153, 156, 158–159, 162–163, 164, 167,
168–169, 170–171, 172–173, 178–179, 181

I want to thank the *Detroit Free Press,* in particular executive editor Heath Meriwether, deputy managing editor Randy Miller, and director of photography Mike Smith, for sending me throughout Eastern Europe to document these events. Their support is deeply appreciated. Special thanks as well to Randy Miller, who helped with the editing, sequencing, and design of the book.

Also at the *Free Press,* thanks to Helen McQuerry, one of the best color printers in the world, and her assistant Diane Bond, for the printing of my photographs in this book. And thanks to John Goecke, Marcia Prouse, Clint Baller, Kenneth Walker, and all of my photographic colleagues at the *Free Press* for their support.

Once again I have had the honor and good fortune of working with president Howard Chapnick and chief picture editor Yukiko Launois of the photographic agency Black Star on this book. They helped with the editing of the photographs and their passion for photojournalism and for humanity is always an inspiration. Black Star distributes my work internationally.

At Stewart, Tabori & Chang, thanks to publisher Andy Stewart, senior editor Maureen Graney, designer Diana Jones, director of production Kathy Rosenbloom, and the staff for their support of this project and for the great care and exquisite quality that goes into the making of their books.

Thanks to Mort Rosenblum, whose spirit is contagious and whose text in this book rekindles the experiences I witnessed throughout Eastern Europe and moved me to tears many times.

Thanks to Bill Garrett, Tom Kennedy, Kent Kobersteen, and the National Geographic staff who helped support my work in Germany and Czechoslovakia.

Thanks to the Associated Press, in particular photographers Greg English and Peter DeJong, and to Reuters for their help throughout Eastern Europe.

Thanks to my colleagues, Jacques Langevin, Derrick Hudson, Chip Hires, Patrick Durand, Eric Bouvet, George Merillon, Anthony Suau, Christopher Morris, Tom Haley, Pierre Hurrel, Chantal De Rudder, Alain Keler, Jim Nachtwey, David Burnett, David Alan Harvey, and countless others for their companionship, courage, and inspiration while covering these events.

Thanks to my brother Peter Turnley, whose photography and compassion I am always inspired by and proud of, and to my family, whose love and support always guides me.

Finally, to my wife Karin, whose love, support, and assistance are my backbone: I thank you from the bottom of my heart.

—David C. Turnley

Peter Turnley

Front cover, 10–11, frontispiece, 16–17,
40–41, 42–43, 49, 50, 54, 57, 58, 60–61,
64–65, 66–67, 68, 70–71, 76–77, 78–79, 80,
82, 83, 84–85, 86–87, 88–89, 94–95, 96,
103, 104, 106–107, 108–109, 110–111, 112,
114–115, 120, 124–125, 126–127, 132–133,
136, 137, 138, 139, 140–141, 142–143, 145,
146–147, 148–149, 150–151, 154–155,
160–161, 165, 166, 174–175, 176–177, 180

I would like to express my gratitude to the
editors of *Newsweek* for sending me on as-
signment to cover the events of Eastern
Europe as they unfolded. Their support of
my work and commitment to photojournalism is deeply appreciated. I want to pay
special thanks to *Newsweek* photo editor
Guy Cooper and international photo editor Hilary Raskin. Their devotion to the
coverage of foreign news and encourage-
ment of my work is a blessing. Thanks to
everyone in the *Newsweek* photo depart-
ment, in particular to art director Patricia
Bradbury and to foreign editor Peter
McGrath.

Howard Chapnick, president of
Black Star, distributes my photos world-
wide; he is a constant inspiration for me.
His elegance and his love for photography
is greatly appreciated. I thank Yukiko
Launois, Ben Chapnick, and everyone at
Black Star.

I would like to thank Andy Stewart
and Maureen Graney, and everyone at
Stewart, Tabori & Chang, for their spirit
and for making this book possible.

I thank former *Newsweek* photo editors Karen Mullarkey and Jim Colton for
their friendship and guidance. *Newsweek*
writers Mike Meyer, Fred Coleman, Carol
Bogert, Rod Nordland, Andrew Nagorski,
Karen Breslau, Chris Dickey, and Ruth
Marshall have all contributed to the spirit
of this book as companions while we reported on the events of Eastern Europe.
Thanks, too, to Jacqueline Duhau, Ginney
Powers, and everyone in *Newsweek*'s Paris
bureau for their help and cooperation.

I thank Mort Rosenblum for his mov-
ing text, for his care for excellence, and for
revealing the human spirit in his reporting.

My brother David, whose work ap-
pears in this book, is a loving friend and
one of my favorite photographers. I thank
my wonderful family for their love and
care for honesty, kindness, and generosity.

—Peter Turnley

DAVID C. TURNLEY (right) has received journalism's top awards for his coverage of Eastern Europe and China: the 1990 Pulitzer Prize in feature photography and the Overseas Press Club Robert Capa Award for work "requiring exceptional courage and enterprise." He also won three citations from the World Press Photo Competition for his work in 1989.

Mr. Turnley, based in Paris for the *Detroit Free Press*, has also photographed for *National Geographic* and been published by *Time, Newsweek,* and *Life.* He won the 1988 World Press Photo Competition's Picture of the Year award, their 1985 Oscar Barnack Award, and previous citations from the Overseas Press Club and University of Missouri and National Press Photographers Canon Essay Award. His previous books, *Why Are They Weeping? South Africans Under Apartheid* (1988) and *Beijing Spring* (1989) were published by Stewart, Tabori & Chang.

PETER TURNLEY'S coverage of the 1989 events in Eastern Europe have also received much praise. His photographs of Nicolae Ceaucescu and the revolution in Romania won the 1990 Overseas Press Club Olivier Rebbot Award for the best photographic reporting from abroad for magazines and books.

A contract photographer for Newsweek, Mr. Turnley has lived in Paris for thirteen years, covering Europe, the Soviet Union, China, Africa, and the Middle East. He has won awards for his previous work from the World Press Photo Competition, the Overseas Press Club, and the NPPA-University of Missouri Pictures of the Year Competition. He has photographed Mikhail Gorbachev more than any other Western photographer. His previous book, *Beijing Spring* (1989), was published by Stewart, Tabori & Chang.

Peter Turnley and his twin brother, David, were born in Indiana. Their photographs are distributed by Black Star.

MORT ROSENBLUM, among the first journalists to arrive in Bucharest after the fall of Ceaucescu, received the 1990 Overseas Press Club Hal Boyle Award in International Reporting for his coverage of Eastern European revolution. A special correspondent for the Associated Press, for which he has worked for twenty-five years, he was also editor-in-chief of the *International Herald Tribune* from 1979 to 1981. He is the author of four previous books, most recently *Back Home: A Foreign Correspondent Rediscovers America.* Mr. Rosenblum is based in Paris.

The type in this book was set in Erhardt and Caslon 224 on the Morgenthaler Linotron 202 at Graphic Arts Composition, Inc., Philadelphia, Pennsylvania, USA.

The book was printed and bound by Toppan Printing Company, Tokyo, Japan.